Original title:
Hedges and Haikus

Copyright © 2025 Creative Arts Management OÜ
All rights reserved.

Author: Milo Harrington
ISBN HARDBACK: 978-1-80566-678-3
ISBN PAPERBACK: 978-1-80566-963-0

Seasonal Thoughts in Syllables

Spring sprouts with glee,
Bunnies hop and sway,
Summer sun sings loud,
Melting ice away.

Leaves dance in the breeze,
Crisp whispers of fall,
Winter chills our toes,
Snowflakes make us crawl.

Serenity Among Sturdy Stocks

Plants friendly and neat,
Petunias laugh bright,
Cutting grass for fun,
Clippings take to flight.

Thorns try to complain,
Yet blooms wink with cheer,
Nature's funny game,
Bringing smiles near.

Meandering Through Verdant Boughs

Along the green maze,
Birds gossip in trees,
Squirrels plan their pranks,
Chasing after bees.

Branches bend and sway,
Tickling the sun,
Nature's silly song,
Has only begun.

Mottled Light and Shade

Dappled sunbeams play,
Chasing shadows round,
Footsteps skip and hop,
With laughter found.

In pockets of green,
Frogs croak loud, alight,
Under growth's warm gaze,
They hop with delight.

A Border of Fleeting Moments

A squirrel steals my snack,
Dancing on the fence,
Chasing its own tail,
Life's a funny pretense.

Ducks play hide and seek,
In the garden's maze,
I trip on my own feet,
Laughter fills the days.

Muted Rhythms in Nature's Thrum

A butterfly flits by,
With a wink, it pirouettes,
I try to impress,
But trip on my own pets.

The frogs croak with pride,
In a not-so-smooth band,
As I dance nearby,
They just don't understand.

Subtle Curves of Green

In tangled vines, I hide,
While the bees zoom and glide,
I strike a silly pose,
But, oh! My shoe's untied.

Laughter drips like dew,
From flowers bright and bold,
Nature's giggles grow,
In colors pure and gold.

Echoes of the Green Enclosure

Leaves rustle with glee,
As I peek and I pounce,
A clumsy cloud-chaser,
In a game I can't flounce.

The robins share a joke,
Between chirps and flutter,
While I'm stuck here, shocked,
In nature's funny clutter.

Lines Written Behind the Arbor

Behind the green, the whispers play,
A squirrel's joke on a sunny day.
Leaves rustle with giggles and cheer,
Nature's punchline, loud and clear.

The bumblebee's dance, a comical sight,
Buzzing in circles, doing it right.
A ladybug tips on a dewy leaf,
"Look at me!" she exclaims with belief.

Peculiar Creatures of the Thicket

A badger with specs reads a tiny book,
His friends all gather for a quick look.
The rabbit complains he's late for lunch,
But someone's left him just a hunch.

Turtles in top hats wear them with flair,
Debating just how to get up in the air.
"A slingshot!" says one with a gleeful grin,
While snails just smile, they're in for the win.

Meditations on a Sunlit Backdrop

In the sunlight, we lounge and dream,
A lizard recites his favorite theme.
The shadows giggle, doing a jig,
As grasshoppers leap, feeling quite big.

A butterfly fluffs up its strange dress,
As ants march in style, they truly impress.
"Did you see that?" the flowers all shout,
"Nature's a circus, without a doubt!"

Echoes from a Bramble's Edge

From thickets arise tales of delight,
Where shadows laugh and creatures take flight.
A fox trips over his own clever toes,
While a wise old owl just watches and knows.

The thorns hum a tune, so wildly fun,
As wrens form a band in the warm sun.
Each note is a chuckle, a wink in the breeze,
Nature's own laughter, with whimsical ease.

In the Curl of Verdant Wisps

A bush in my yard,
It dances with grace,
Caterpillars party,
In the leafy embrace.

Squirrels throw acorns,
And giggle a tune,
As birds join the chorus,
Under the bright moon.

Verses Cradled by Greenery

In the thicket so deep,
A frog jumps with glee,
He croaks out a sonnet,
To a passing bee.

The mushrooms are laughing,
With their caps in the air,
They twirl in the twilight,
Without a single care.

Whispers of Green Foliage

A patch of wild weeds,
Plotting cheerful schemes,
They're sharing gossip,
In the sun's golden beams.

Tangled vines gossip,
In their playful tease,
While bunnies make mischief,
In the rustling leaves.

A Form of Silent Growth

In corners of gardens,
Little plots play shy,
With tomatoes giggling,
As the peas flutter by.

The mint's got a secret,
Whispered soft in the breeze,
While cabbages chuckle,
Waving tiny green sleeves.

Ponderings on Guarded Spaces

In the corner they grow,
Watching folks pass by,
Whispers of mischief,
And the cat's sly eye.

Oh, the secrets they keep,
Like a gossiping friend,
Peeking through the leaves,
Around every bend.

Are they hiding a treasure,
Or just lost in thought?
Maybe dreaming of snacks,
Or what can be sought.

With a snicker they sway,
As the wind pulls a prank,
While we laugh at their tales,
In the green, leafy bank.

Tenderness Among the Twigs

Little branches entwined,
In a dance of delight,
A party of twigs,
In the warm golden light.

Whispers of sweetness,
In each twitch and turn,
And the ants join the fun,
With their job to discern.

Oh, the shenanigans cease,
When a squirrel rolls by,
Making friends with a leaf,
Tossed up to the sky.

With laughter a flutter,
Nature's funny parade,
All twisted together,
In antics they made.

Flickers of Dawn Through the Foliage

Morning sun peeks in,
With a grin on its face,
Tickling every leaf,
In a warm embrace.

The shadows are dancing,
With a skip and a shake,
While the bugs plan a rave,
For the dawn's gentle wake.

A robin sings out loud,
With a sparkle of cheer,
While the berries giggle,
As they burst into spheres.

In this playful world,
Where the sun starts to bloom,
It's a festival of joy,
In a leafy green room.

Subtle Echoes of Nature's Voice

Listen closely, my friend,
To the leaves' little chats,
They mumble and giggle,
Like a troupe of old bats.

Each rustle and murmur,
A story untold,
Of the critters that dance,
And the wondrous and bold.

A frog croaks a tune,
In a croaky delight,
While the flowers just blush,
In their colorful plight.

In the calm of the woods,
Where the giggles arise,
Nature's laughter is heard,
Under twinkling skies.

Darting Shadows and Rustling Dreams

Beneath the leafy shade, they peep,
Tiny critters dance and leap.
A squirrel does a little prance,
While grasshoppers take their chance.

Laughter hides in tangled vines,
Mischief wrapped in twirling lines.
A wily fox wears quite the grin,
As he plots where to begin.

Sunbeams tickle the hidden ground,
While shadows play, they leap around.
Each nook and cranny is a stage,
For the antics of the age.

Giggles rustle through the bramble,
Life's a game, a cheeky gamble.
So come and join this folly fair,
With secrets waiting everywhere!

Poems from the Fingered Fronds

In leafy arms, the whispers dance,
Each flick and flutter begs a chance.
Nature giggles, what a sight,
As twigs and twirls take flight each night.

Fingers stretch, in playful bows,
Tickling leaves as laughter flows.
Beetles hum in silly song,
A cacophony where we belong.

A frog in night attire croaks,
While fireflies engage in jokes.
The ferns sway, swish with glee,
As if they're laughing back at me.

Join the fandango, skip and run,
In forests thick, where jokes are spun.
Beneath the fronds, we laugh and play,
Until the dawn steals night away!

Watching Wisps of Cloud Above

Clouds gather like a fluffy crew,
Wearing hats of every hue.
A pirate ship floats past in jest,
While a dragon snoozes, quite the rest.

Painted skies hold cloud parade,
As rainbows tease, they laugh and fade.
Giggling pillows drift and sway,
In a cotton-candy ballet.

Kites in disguise float near to play,
As dreams weave stories they can say.
A band of giggles fills the blue,
With whispers soft that feel so true.

When twilight beckons, stars will twinkle,
In the crowd of clouds, there's joy to sprinkle.
Whether high or low, we'll chant and cheer,
Life's a jest, come join, my dear!

Encounters with the Breezy Frame

A dash of wind stirs up the fun,
It tickles cheeks, a cheeky run.
With swirling skirts, it takes your hat,
Now you're chasing, imagine that!

Wavy grasses bend and bow,
Breezy breath, like a gentle vow.
Each gust carries a giggle strong,
As nature dances to its song.

Trees sway low, they're joining in,
A gusty waltz beneath the din.
Pine cones tumble, giggling loud,
In this frolicsome, playful crowd.

Grab your joy, let's play the game,
In this frame, we'll stake our claim.
With each swirl and each nudge of air,
Laughs cascade, for we shall share!

The Lingering Aroma of Earth

The soil has secrets,
Like squirrels with nuts.
Aroma of damp moss,
And childhood's little cuts.

A worm wriggles by,
Shiny and quite proud.
It dances in circles,
As if it's in a crowd.

Snails hide in their shells,
In a slow-motion race.
They've got a fast life,
But can't quite keep pace.

The rain taps a tune,
On leaves like a drum.
Nature's comedy show,
With no ticket, just fun.

Scattered Verses on the Ground

A leaf falls softly,
Landing with a flap.
It tells tales of autumn,
And whispers of a nap.

The grass tickles toes,
In a joyful embrace.
While ants march in lines,
At a determined pace.

A ladybug winks,
With polka dots galore.
Fashion icon of bugs,
Always wanting more.

Wind laughs through the trees,
With jokes we can't hear.
Leaves giggle and sway,
In a front-row seat cheer.

Speckles of Inspiration in the Thicket

In the thicket so wild,
Ideas sprout and creep.
Like rabbits in the night,
Quite crafty, but cheap.

A frog croaks a joke,
Though no one can laugh.
It ribbits on rhythm,
A true wordsmith's gaffe.

Dandelions puff,
Like tiny clouds of fluff.
They make wishes float,
But they never are tough.

The bushes eavesdrop,
On whispers and schemes.
They chuckle in green,
As they nurture our dreams.

Billowing Dreams Amidst the Green

Clouds wear pretentious hats,
Like they own the sky.
They drift with big egos,
While we softy sigh.

Butterflies gossip,
In colors so bright.
They flutter their wings,
In a delicate flight.

The breeze plays a prank,
On the tall, swaying grass.
It shimmies and shakes,
Watch those blades all sass!

With laughter and joy,
Nature plots with the sun.
In this whimsical world,
Every moment is fun.

Lush Encounters at the Threshold

In a garden so wide,
A squirrel stole my shoe,
I chased him through thorns,
He laughed as he flew.

Trailing blooms on my path,
I tripped on a vine,
The rabbit just grinned,
Sipping tea like divine.

With each step I take,
The gnomes start to dance,
They wave little hands,
To a goblin's romance.

Next to muddy old boots,
A worm in a tie,
"Care for a dance?"
"Only under the sky!"

The Silence Between the Blooms

Where bees talk in whispers,
And flowers debate,
A rose insists it's red,
While daisies just wait.

Beneath skies of laughter,
A tulip winks light,
"I'm taller than you,"
"Not if it's not night!"

The wind flutters close,
With secrets it brings,
A gossiping fern,
That says "My, oh my!"

Between petals and leaves,
We giggle and grin,
The garden's our stage,
Let the fun times begin!

Tucked Away in the Green

In the shade of the shrubs,
A frog made a throne,
With lilies for fans,
He croaks all alone.

A snail with a hat,
Wonders where he should roam,
"Why is life so slow?"
"Because you're at home!"

Chasing shadows of flies,
The grasshoppers jump,
They take bets on each dive,
With a comedic thump.

Whispers in the glow,
Of a hedgehog at play,
"Don't touch my nice hat!"
"It's a fine day today!"

Fragments of a Secret Grove

In a nook of the shade,
Grows a not-so-fine grape,
Bubbles rare laughter,
Not quite a cape!

Mice tell their tall tales,
Of cheese made from hair,
While shadows do pirouettes,
In the cool morning air.

Each twig hides a giggle,
A spade shared with dreams,
While crickets compose,
Their silly moonbeams.

Underneath leafy chatters,
Are whispers and cheese,
"Next time bring a dance!"
"A round of good cheese!"

The Song of Interrupting Leaves

A leaf drops down,
Plops right on my shoe.
"Excuse me, sir!" it shouts,
"You're blocking my view!"

The tree holds its breath,
Curtains of green sway.
Squirrels practice ballet,
While the branches play.

Sunlight tries to sneak,
Through gaps in the zest.
The branches comically,
Frown like they're stressed.

Leaves giggle and dance,
In a playful spree.
Nature's own pranks,
Just for you and me.

Reflections at the Boundary

A bush with a grin,
Winks as I walk by.
"No peeking tonight!"
It puffs up its sigh.

The fence keeps on creaking,
It's worn and it's old.
Sharing secrets,
That never get told.

A gnome with a smirk,
Looks out from the weeds.
Straw hat full of dreams,
Its luck never leads.

The path sways and bends,
In a curious drift.
Nature plays tricks,
With a whimsical gift.

Breath of the Botanical Veil

In the garden's heart,
Roses start to gossip.
"Who wore it best?" they ask,
While petals just slip.

A butterfly giggles,
Donning a new style.
"Gotta keep it fresh,
You know, just for a while!"

The daisies all chuckle,
In a crowd so bright.
"Let's have a dance-off,
Under the moonlight!"

Laughter fills the air,
With each bloom they shake.
A garden soirée,
For the fun of it, make!

Verses Nestled in Positioned Shrubs

Between green curtains,
Whispers float along.
"Did you hear that one?"
"Oh, tell me, it's long!"

A willow sneezes loud,
Leaves scatter like confetti.
"Achoo!" it declares,
"My branches are sweaty!"

Tiny critters chuckle,
In their leafy lair.
"Did you spot the cat?"
"Oh no, we should beware!"

The bushes orchestrate,
A tune of pure jest.
Nature's sweet laughter,
Ensuring we're blessed.

Tranquil Borders of Thought

In the garden, thoughts bloom bright,
Branches dance in morning light.
Bees are buzzing, laughter sings,
Nature's joy in simple things.

Worms debate under the shade,
Tangled tales in whispers laid.
A squirrel juggling acorns here,
While birds chirp, spreading cheer.

Frogs recite their little rhymes,
In puddles, they perform at times.
With leafy hats, they take a bow,
Foliage laughs—let's join them now!

Tiny worlds in vibrant green,
Hidden wonders, rarely seen.
If walls could talk, oh the jest,
In this green realm, we are blessed!

Verse Beneath the Boughs

Whispers rise from leaf-strewn ground,
Boughs above, a playful round.
Chirping crickets share their dreams,
Sprouting giggles, giggly beams.

Ants dance on their busy trails,
While laughter floats on gentle gales.
In shadowed corners, secrets hide,
Where nature's jokes cannot be tried.

The old oak grins, a wise old sage,
While vines weave stories page by page.
Beneath the canopy's embrace,
We find a smile in nature's grace.

A rabbit hops, a playful tease,
While bumblebees just aim to please.
In this tangled tapestry, we jest,
With every breath, we're nature's guests!

Secrets of the Overgrown

In the thicket, tales unfold,
Clovers hiding treasures bold.
Grasshoppers leap with such delight,
In this jungle, day turns night.

A lizard waves, a small parade,
Blades of grass, the perfect shade.
Hedgerows giggle in the breeze,
With every sway, they aim to please.

Mushrooms sprout like tiny hats,
While the chubby toad just chats.
With blooming blooms, they prank the eye,
In this green world, laughter's high.

Every twist and turn reveals,
A subtle jest the forest steals.
Join the fun, take off your frown,
In the wild's arms, let joy abound!

The Quiet Protest of Foliage

Leaves in protest, gently sway,
Shouting softly, 'Come and play!'
The underbrush, a crowded crowd,
With whispers floating, brave and loud.

Petals blush, like kids in class,
Bright colors waving as they pass.
A hedgehog prances with a grin,
In nature's riot, joy begins.

Squirrels strike poses on the line,
With acorn hats, feeling divine.
Each twig and sprout holds wisdom keen,
In this calm uproar, life unseen.

The laughter swells beneath the sun,
As branches bend, behold the fun!
In leafy realms where giggles float,
Nature's mischief, a joyful quote!

Shimmering Borders

Tiny bugs like dancers,
Waltzing on the green stage.
Tickled by a breezy wind,
They zigzag, laugh, and engage.

Sunlight plays peek-a-boo,
With shadows stretched so wide.
A squirrel steals my sandwich,
I chase but can't abide.

Bouncing leaves dive for cover,
From prying eyes above.
A gentle breeze whispers down,
While I just want some grub.

In these borders of delight,
Life's a picnic, what a sight!
With chaos all around me,
I grin, it feels so right.

Nature's Whispered Edges

At the cusp of branches sway,
A chorus sings each day.
Birds dressed in wacky hues,
Tweet soft jokes to amuse.

A bumblebee's grand blunder,
Dives headlong toward a flower.
With petals full of laughter,
It buzzes, flops, and cowers.

The grass tickles my toes,
As I dance in clumsy glee.
I trip over a sneaky root,
Nature giggles at me.

In these edges, life's a game,
Where giggles always reign.
We frolic through the shrubby maze,
And join in nature's playful refrain.

Verses by the Garden Path

Dandelions wear their crowns,
As the sun begins to fade.
A frog croaks its finest tune,
On the lily pad parade.

Bunny hops with giddy flair,
Nibbles on a sprig of thyme.
Next to him, a sneaky snail,
Says, "I'll beat you, just in time!"

All the flowers giggle bright,
Whispering in soft delight.
A squirrel steals a garden hat,
Claiming it his new invite.

Each twist and turn along the way,
Brings laughter, light, and play.
In this seeming chaos found,
We find joy all around.

Shadows of the Leafy Realm

Beneath the leafy canopy,
Where light and giggles blend.
A shadow slips, a playful tease,
As dancing leaves descend.

A raccoon trots with sass,
Balancing on a fence.
With every trip and tumble,
It makes the day intense.

The breeze has jokes to share,
Tickling flowers as they bloom.
As petals shake in laughter,
Their fragrance fills the room.

In this leafy realm of cheer,
Where butterflies draw near,
We've crafted our own silly song,
With laughter and good cheer.

Stanzas of the Untamed Edge

In the garden, things grow wild,
Squirrels host a dance, oh so styled.
Rabbits hop in jazzy cheer,
Whiskers twitching, no sign of fear.

Frogs wear crowns made of small twigs,
Chanting songs, doing funny jigs.
Grasshoppers leap with flair and grace,
While ants march on, keeping pace.

Each flower holds a secret laugh,
Bees buzz by, sharing a gaffe.
With petals bright, they tease the sun,
In this lively plot, they have their fun.

Nature's punchlines make us grin,
Wit in blooms is where we begin.
So listen close, dear friend of mine,
In this wild world, humor's divine.

Breezes Sing in the Thicket

Whistles weave through the leafy maze,
Breezy shouts in a playful haze.
The trees chuckle, their trunks in sync,
Sharing tales with the clouds, I think.

Birds debate who's the best at song,
Chirping loudly, they can't be wrong.
An owl rolls its eyes, and takes a nap,
While a cheeky crow sets a prank-filled trap.

Vines twist together in gossipy cheer,
Laughter echoes, bringing us near.
The bushes gossip, sharing a glance,
Even the stones seem to join in the dance.

So come play in this thicket around,
Where silliness sprouts from the ground.
Nature's comedy makes the heart sing,
In this joyful place, hilarity is king.

Reflections from a Hidden Path

Around the bend, a squirrel does plot,
With acorns in hand, the clever little tot.
A raccoon peeks from a shadowy nook,
With a grin that could catch any crook.

Under leaves where light only glows,
A ladybug jests, and everyone knows.
Hidden in charms and soft forest breeze,
Nature's whispers bring giggles with ease.

Mushrooms giggle at passing feet,
Tickled by moss, their laughter's a treat.
Paths lined with ferns play games of hide,
While chipmunks cheer from the sideline, wide-eyed.

So step with care, and don't be shy,
These woods are alive, oh my oh my!
With punchy jests and a spark of glee,
Every nook in this path holds a chuckle for thee.

The Art of Leafy Pauses

In the flicker of leaves, a joke is spun,
As two squirrel friends have a sneaky run.
They leap and tumble, oh what a sight,
Making mischief, hearts feeling light.

Each pause reveals a hidden jest,
While beetles play cards, who's the best?
A wily fox grins, tail waving proud,
As all of nature gathers, a humorous crowd.

The air is thick with chortles and glee,
As nature's jesters embrace the spree.
Flowers shake with laughter so free,
In this leafy circus, come join, take a seat!

So let's celebrate each chuckle and cheer,
In the art of laughter, we hold dear.
With every pause, the joy increases,
In this merry realm, where humor never ceases.

A Tapestry of Twigs

Whispers of branches sway,
Laughter hides in the leaves,
Bouncing squirrels in the fray,
Nature's mischief deceives.

Mossy hats on gnomes wear,
Dancing with chubby bees,
Jellybeans tumble where,
Bugs share jokes in the breeze.

Colors clash, a painter's dream,
Dandelions sprout with flair,
Each blade grass a vibrant scheme,
Twirling tales beyond compare.

Tickling edges of the yard,
Twinkle toes on the logs,
Little hearts beat real hard,
In the kingdom of frogs.

Syllables Woven in Green

Leaves giggle in the sun,
Whispering secrets unheard,
Round and round, nature's fun,
Each leaf is a clever bird.

Ducks in boots paddle by,
Crickets sing silly tunes,
With a hop and a shy,
They dance beneath the moons.

Tiny toads wear little crowns,
Rabbits throw a tea party,
Juggling their carrot downs,
Chasing dreams quite hearty.

In this patch of delight,
Watch the shadows play games,
Their laughter takes flight,
A world without the same names.

Rustling Thoughts Behind the Shrub

Behind the bush, whispers thrill,
A ladybug dons a cape,
With every tiny chill,
She plans her grand escape.

Ants at work, hatching schemes,
Wily and quick on their feet,
Wrestling with chocolate dreams,
A feast none could defeat.

Grassy floors, velvet soft,
Chasing reflections of light,
Bonsai card tricks aloft,
Nature's magic in sight.

Behind the leafy curtain,
A world of giggles awaits,
Each little laugh uncertain,
Amid fantastic debates.

Serenity Shaped by Branches

In treetops, dreams take flight,
Napping under a warm haze,
Caterpillars write at night,
With pencils made of rays.

Bees wear crowns of sweet gold,
Making honey from laughter,
In the garden, tales unfold,
Silliness after disaster.

Rabbits boast of the race,
With quirks that baffle and thrill,
A frolic in leafy space,
Funny faces, giggles spill.

In every shadow and nook,
Small adventures wave and greet,
With each corner, take a look,
Life is life's sweetest treat.

Latticework of Shadows

In the garden we giggle,
As the gnarled branches wiggle.
A squirrel tries yoga,
Tripping on a tumbleweed.

Sunbeams play peek-a-boo,
Chasing shadows that construe.
A bird thinks it's a star,
But it's just the dog's loud bark.

Fluffy clouds float above,
Whispering secrets of love.
The grass starts to dance,
Caught in nature's sweet trance.

Behind the fence they say,
Lies the biggest game of play.
But all I see is mud,
Should have brought my yellow boots.

In the Shade of Thoughtful Growth

Under leafy canopies,
The ants hold conferences.
Debating which crumb's best,
While I munch on popcorn zest.

Beneath the sprawling leaves,
Nature forms wild reprieves.
A frog croaks a joke loud,
The lily pads drew a crowd.

Petunias start a band,
With daisies lending a hand.
But when the wind comes by,
Every petal takes to the sky.

In this patchwork of green,
Misfits thrive, unheard, unseen.
Each giggle, an echo,
Of fun where wildflowers grow.

Words Among the Leafy Fringe

In the shrubbery's embrace,
We find the silliest face.
A raccoon in a tie,
Waving 'hello' with a sigh.

The daisies tell tall tales,
Of the snail's long-winded scales.
While butterflies assist,
With stories they can't resist.

Whispers float on the breeze,
As the old oak cracks a tease.
The petals turn to giggle,
As the wind begins to wiggle.

Amid the flurry of green,
Laughter plays, unseen, serene.
Words hang like ripe fruit,
But the squirrels are quick to loot.

Fleeting Images Behind the Brush

A brushstroke here, a splash there,
The garden spills out a flair.
Bees buzz like tiny cars,
Chasing after glistening stars.

Hidden sprites have their fun,
Racing raindrops, one by one.
Each flicker brings delight,
As the dawn swallows the night.

A cat peeks through the gloom,
Decides it's no longer boom.
Swatting at shadows near,
It mistook them for a deer.

Behind the tangled vines,
A cheeky rabbit outlines.
With each hop, a clumsy dance,
Sprinkling laughter with every prance.

Fluttering Thoughts at Dusk

A butterfly lands near,
Daring the evening breeze.
It flutters past my ear,
With nonsense and a tease.

Whispers of the leaves sway,
As shadows start to grin.
They play their secret game,
Where giggles softly spin.

A crow laughs at my hat,
Misplaced upon my head.
I wonder if it's that,
Or just my daily bread.

The stars peek from the fog,
As night wears shades of gray.
A giggling little frog,
Croaks jokes till break of day.

Surrounded by Living Edges

In a jungle of twigs,
Where squirrels plan a heist.
They stash acorns in digs,
And laugh at their own feist.

A hedgehog with a grin,
Rolls into a bright ball.
He knows he'll win again,
In this quirky sprawl.

Vines dance in the breeze,
While flowers play tag too.
They rustle with such ease,
Like kids on a good cue.

Around the sharp corners,
With laughter and delight.
Nature's playground borne,
In shadows full of light.

Crooked Lines of Growth

A twig with dreams of height,
Leans sideways with a smile.
Claiming its unique sight,
In its own crooked style.

Grass tries to race the sun,
But trips on a loose root.
It laughs, knowing the fun,
Of living in pursuit.

A worm slips, giving chase,
In muddy, joyful haste.
Tripping in its own race,
It wriggles with such taste.

Around the twisting bends,
A tea party awaits.
Where laughter never ends,
And joy dictates the fates.

Botanicals in Verse

Cactus wearing a hat,
Pokes fun at a blue jay.
Through spikes, a little spat,
Leaves laughter on display.

A daisy shows its teeth,
With petals bright and wide.
It sings a tune of heath,
Always on the fun side.

The lilies share a wink,
With bubbles in their bloom.
While frogs all start to think,
Of how to lift the gloom.

In gardens of delight,
Where every flower sings.
The night takes off in flight,
And dances with the springs.

Whispers Among the Green

In the garden's cozy nook,
Gossiping flowers take a look.
They share secrets, rich and bold,
While the lazy sun turns gold.

A squirrel tries to sneak a snack,
But the daisies launch an attack.
"Hey, you thief with a fluffy tail!"
Laughter echoes without fail.

The hedgehog rolls, a furry ball,
He joins the chat with a gentle sprawl.
"Is it me, or did the grass just grow?"
Cheerful banter, stealing the show.

A bumblebee buzzes, oh so grand,
Dropping punchlines to the band.
The petals shimmy, laughing out loud,
Nature's comedy, vibrant and proud.

Seasons in a Leafy Frame

Spring arrives with a silly prank,
Blossoms dance on the riverbank.
"Watch out!" shouts a windblown leaf,
"I've got jokes, no room for grief!"

Summer breezes come in quick,
Setting up for a comic trick.
Frogs in shades sip lemonade,
While fireflies make a disco parade.

Autumn chuckles, leaves on the ground,
Sweater weather's got all around.
A crow quips, as he's taking flight,
"More like 'fowl' weather tonight!"

Winter's frost brings the frosty fun,
Snowmen bow when the day is done.
A snowflake slips, slips on a sled,
And the whole forest laughs instead.

Shadows in the Serene

The shadows stretch, giggling wide,
As the sun takes a leisurely ride.
A cat sprawls on the garden wall,
Whispers to the clouds—"I'm the boss of all!"

A ladybug spots a sunning snail,
"You're slow, but your humor's not stale!"
Together they ponder life's little tease,
While the daisies sway with the breeze.

The breeze tickles, and the trees reply,
With swaying limbs and a flirty sigh.
They trade tall tales and silly myths,
About dancing mushrooms and playful drifts.

Even the stones join in on the spree,
With rock-solid jokes, as stiff as can be.
In the garden, shadows hold a sway,
With laughter echoing all through the day.

Nature's Silent Barriers

The bushes gossip, heads held high,
"Silly squirrel! Think you can fly?"
They shake with laughter, rustle with glee,
While the critters watch, as happy as can be.

A fence of twigs, too proud to bow,
Mocks the patches of flourished sow.
"I guard the peas, I'm quite the sight!"
But they all know he's scared of the night.

A rabbit hops with a cheeky grin,
"The grass is greener, let's sneak in!"
But the nettle's sting has a funny sting,
The garden's charm is a wondrous thing.

In this realm where nature plays,
Every barrier brings funny displays.
With whispers, chuckles, and warm embraces,
Life unfolds in joyous spaces.

Emotional Thickets

In tangled thoughts we roam,
Lost like socks, far from home.
A squirrel giggles at our plight,
As we fumble in twilight.

Bushes whisper with some cheer,
"Hey, don't take yourselves too near!"
We stumble over roots with glee,
Nature's jesters: wild and free.

Each twist, a surprise in store,
Like finding snacks behind the door.
We laugh at the mess we've made,
In our emotional charade.

Who knew a thicket could bring fun?
Like a comedy, just begun.
With every branch and twig in tow,
We dance where the wild winds blow.

An Invitation Behind the Shrubs

Underneath the leafy cloak,
A sign awaits: 'Let's have a joke!'
Come venture where the shadows play,
We'll giggle 'til the end of day.

Beneath the fronds, a party brews,
With ants that march in little shoes.
A rabbit leaves his carrot stake,
To join the silliness we make.

Your invitation, it's quite absurd,
From a chatty, gossiping bird.
By the shrubs, let laughter bound,
Such mirth in the thicket found!

So grab your hat and wear a grin,
Let the merry fracas begin.
For life is short, and so divine,
Let's frolic 'neath the tangled vine.

Stanzas Hidden Beneath the Canopy

In the shade of wordy trees,
Where whispers tickle like a breeze.
Puns and riddles all around,
Laughter echoing, joy abound.

Branches stretching, verse in rise,
Nature's laughter, oh, so wise.
Twisted lines and funny rhymes,
We scribble jokes and nicknames, chimes.

The sun peeks through with playful glee,
Playing hopscotch with the bees.
Each stanza like a hop or skip,
Where humor takes a tiny trip.

So come along, do not be shy,
Under this canopy, we'll fly.
With laughter woven in our thread,
We'll craft a tale, where fun is spread.

Fragments of Nature's Secrets

Amidst the leaves, we sneak and spy,
On gossipers that flit and fly.
A secret here, a secret there,
Like searching for a lost old chair.

Tiny creatures in a fuss,
Chattering about all of us.
With every rustle, every laugh,
We find the fun within the path.

Fragments shared beneath the sky,
Nature's giggles, oh, so spry.
Here a chuckle, there a snort,
In the thicket, life's a sport!

So let's embrace this joyful quest,
Where humor thrives and we are blessed.
In nature's arms, we'll find our cue,
To laugh at secrets, old and new.

The Language of Trimmed Greens

In gardens where bushes grin,
Whispers of leaves, a cheeky spin.
Weathered pruners dance with glee,
As shrubs plot their next decree.

With snips and clips, the gossip spreads,
Rumors push through patchy threads.
'Who will be topiary king?'
Bouncing jokes on a leafy swing.

Fragrant blooms roll their eyes,
While shorn brambles tell no lies.
"Look at me, so neat and spry!"
But tangled roots just smile and sigh.

A dandelion laughs so loud,
Poking fun at the primmed and proud.
"Who's the best in this leafy race?"
While weeds just love to take up space.

Enclosed in Nature's Embrace

A vine-swayed dance, what a sight,
Tickled by shadows, day and night.
Whiskers of grass poke out to play,
Telling secrets in their own way.

Petals smirk at the snooty trees,
Challenging roots with a light breeze.
"What's elegance in a funky twist?"
While creeping moss just can't resist.

Chirps and chortles in the thick brush,
Squirrels giggle, in a rush.
"Who knew that shrubs held such delight?"
As they frolic under moonlight.

Boundaries blur, a funny scene,
Where nature thrives, so wild and green.
"Join our party, let's create a fuss!"
And the branches sway with rustling trust.

Pauses in the Leafy Labyrinth

In corners where sunlight barely glows,
A quirky maze, where no one goes.
Twisting paths with no clear aim,
Whispers teasing, "What's your name?"

The ferns giggle, their fronds in cheer,
"Lost again? Come gather here!"
A snail ambles, with royal pace,
"Patience, dear friend, it's quite the race."

Ticklish tendrils tickle your toes,
Hiding from what nobody knows.
"Mystery awaits at every bend,"
Shrubbery grins, "Let's pretend!"

Around the bend, a bunny hops,
Bounding past with comedic flops.
"Where's the exit?" they curiously ask,
But enjoy the puzzle, a joyful task!

Symmetry in the Underbrush

Leafy forms in a fun parade,
A jolly mix, where art is made.
"Who's that squished by the hedgerow?"
Laughter echoes—"Let's not stop the show!"

Barks and branches lay out their game,
Crooked lines with a dash of fame.
"Look at my potpourri of tones!"
While butterflies wave their funny phones.

"In the chaos, there's a grand scheme,"
Silly little vibes flow like a dream.
"Perfectly crooked, that's the art,"
Nature chuckles, "plans fall apart!"

Oddities dance, a merry play,
As flowers bloom in bright array.
"Join the riot, let's be absurd,"
For the underbrush is never deterred.

Nature's Soft Embrace

In the garden's arms, so wide,
Socks on my hands, no place to hide.
Weird little critters leap and frolic,
Nature laughs, it's quite symbolic.

Worms wear top hats, worms wear coats,
They're throwing a party, and yes, it floats!
The daisies are dancing, grass is too,
Even the rocks join in the view!

Sunlight winks from behind a tree,
I bet it knows, just wait and see.
A leaf whispers jokes to a passing breeze,
And squirrels chuckle as they tease.

Ode to the flowers, colorful and bright,
Mocking the wind with all their might.
In this soft embrace, joy's never far,
Embraced by laughter, nature's bizarre!

Clusters of Comfort and Space

Pillows piled up, a fortress made,
I sit inside, a grand charade.
Blankets like clouds, soft as a dream,
Imagination's vessel, or so it seems.

Popcorn armies fight with candy ships,
Chocolate rivers spill from crumbly lips.
Lollipop trees and gumdrop hills,
Worry takes flight; the laughter spills.

Every corner holds a giggling friend,
A runaway joke we'll never send.
Cushions vibrant, laughter's embrace,
Giggles and grins in our secret space.

Climbing the towers with giggling ease,
A kingdom of comfort as sweet as cheese.
In this cluster, joy gets to race,
Together we thrive, in our happy place!

Quietly Cultivated Thoughts

Sowing ideas in my mind's plot,
Seeds of laughter, and others forgot.
Foot-tall plans, but short on sense,
Measuring mirth, and building suspense.

Watering whims with a splashy grin,
Pruning the clumsy, let the fun begin.
Fertilize joy with a pinch of cheer,
And watch as the giggles start to appear.

While weeds of worry grow tall and wide,
I simply dance, with dreams as my guide.
Butterflies tend the flowers of thought,
Reaping the joy that laughter has brought.

In silence I gather the fresh delight,
Weaving my whimsy, morning to night.
Cultivated clearly, with peace interspersed,
Thoughts quietly bloom, like bubbles dispersed.

The Poetry of Boundaries

In the garden fence, a tale untold,
Where jokes are shared and secrets unfold.
A line defined, yet spirits take flight,
Growing together, a dazzling sight.

The perimeter's charm lies in its mess,
Boundaries blur when giggles impress.
With each little flower, a barrier bends,
Celebrating play, where laughter transcends.

Scribbles of madness on a clay-dirt page,
Laughter erupts, freeing each cage.
Between the lines, the wit comes alive,
Amidst juicy satire, we joyfully thrive.

So cheers to the borders, where we may frolic,
Adding bright colors, oh how symbolic!
In boundaries defined, we find our grace,
In this quirky life, there's always space!

Tiny Worlds in Overgrown Corners

In tangled greens so wild and spry,
A worm's grand race, oh my, oh my!
A ladybug on a leaf does pirouette,
While ants play poker, a risky bet.

A thistle whispers secrets near,
To jolly old toads filled with cheer.
They chuckle 'bout flies that dance and tease,
While snails slide slow, with elegant ease.

A rabbit hops with little care,
Bounding through grass like it's a lair.
Each nook and cranny holds such delight,
Where critters laugh into the night.

With every rustle and gentle sway,
Nature plays games in light-hearted play.
The corner grows, with every blink,
Tiny worlds—what do they think?

The Art of Nature's Privacy

Behind green walls where whispers dwell,
The shyest flowers form a cell.
A tucked-away space with giggles inside,
Where beetles peek, taking pride.

A fence of leaves keeps secrets tight,
As squirrels perform in the fading light.
They strut around in flashy coats,
Avoiding noise that simply gloats.

Here, ants plan a grand escape,
While dragonflies dress up in drape.
A dance of shadows, a waltz of bees,
Nature conceals her quirks with ease.

The art of hiding, oh what a game,
With every rustle, it's never the same.
If only we could join their spree,
In their green world, wild and free.

Soft Murmurs in Leafy Edges

Amidst the leaves, soft giggles rise,
As squirrels plot their wild, wise guys.
Chirps of crickets, a late-night tune,
While owls nod to a sleepy moon.

A patchwork quilt of greens and grays,
Where butterflies frolic on bright sun rays.
A sneaky fox dons a cloak of art,
Stealing glimpses, playing the part.

Fluffy clouds whisper jokes to trees,
As shadows tango in the gentle breeze.
The fun unfurls with a flick and leap,
Awakening giggles from slumber deep.

In nature's realm, laughter strikes bold,
In soft murmurings, life unfolds.
With glee we watch, no need to pretend,
In leafy corners, joy finds no end.

Hushed Confessions of the Garden

In the twilight hours, secrets bloom,
As daisies giggle, dispelling gloom.
Petals blush with a knowing wink,
While shadows play and creatures think.

A busy bee shares tales of delight,
Of garden gossip under stars so bright.
With buzzing laughter that lifts the ground,
In each soft sigh, joy is found.

Underneath the moon's soft glow,
Frogs debate where the best bugs go.
They croak and chuckle, a comedic pair,
In this hidden world, humor fills the air.

Confessions whispered, so silly and sweet,
Nature's own jesters, life's little treats.
In the hush of the night, let laughter reign,
In the garden's heart, joy will remain.

The Edge of Stillness

At the border of calm, a frog starts to croak,
A tree starts to giggle at the old garden yoke.
Bewitched by the quiet, I stumble and trip,
Is that a squirrel laughing, or a leaf's little quip?

A snail in a shell tells secrets to air,
While ants hold a meeting, without any care.
The breeze whispers jokes, or so it seems,
Nature's odd humor hides in its dreams.

Echoes of Leaves Unturned

Whispers fly by as the branches all sway,
A worm writes a novel, but it can't find a way.
With every soft rustle, I chuckle anew,
Is the grass trying to tickle, or is it just dew?

A butterfly's laughter, a spider's sly grin,
Each critter is plotting another little sin.
The sun's rays peek out, oh what a surprise,
They wink at the clouds as they gather their ties.

Lost in the Thicket's Embrace

In the maze of green, I play hide and seek,
With a bush full of berries, oh what a cheek!
A chubby raccoon steals my last cookie,
While I chuckle softly, oh life's such a kooky!

Branches like arms wrap around with great cheer,
They tickle my sides, making giggles appear.
The world spins in circles, I can't find my way,
But the laughter of nature is here to stay!

The Poetry of Pruned Dreams

Chopped down but sprightly, the branches now dance,
Roots stuck in the past, but they dream and they prance.
In the garden's embrace, a cat takes a nap,
While daisies hold meetings to plot their next flap.

With scissors and laughter, a gardener scripts,
A story of growth that gives nature quips.
As petals fall down, like confetti in spring,
They giggle in chaos, oh, what joy they bring!

Intricacies of Nature's Palette

Leaves dance in the breeze,
Colors blend in perfect tease.
There's a squirrel doing ballet,
While the birds shout, "Hey! It's okay!"

In the grass, a bug winks,
Caterpillars debate over drinks.
A flower giggles, it's true,
A bee buzzes, just passing through.

Twigs hold a secret meeting,
Roots are there, quietly greeting.
Nature's paint spills on the ground,
Across this canvas, joy is found.

The ants form a tiny parade,
Marching strong, but slightly delayed.
Nature's stage where all are bold,
A painted jest, a sight to behold.

A Quiet Meditation at Day's End

The sun yawns, sinking low,
Shadows stretch, putting on a show.
A frog croaks a wise old tale,
While fireflies twinkle like a trail.

Grass blades whisper, secrets shared,
As crickets play, none are scared.
A mouse peeks from a leafy nook,
Once shy, it now takes a look.

The wind chuckles, tickling leaves,
Nature's humor, it weaves and weaves.
Stars emerge, with a wink at best,
As day turns into a feathered jest.

In the air, laughter is spun,
A soft farewell to the sun.
With each dusk, stories unwind,
Nature's grin leaves joy behind.

Delicate Secrets in the Understory

Beneath the trees, a world so small,
Dancing mushrooms, a tiny ball.
A beetle dons a shiny suit,
While worms gather to play their flute.

Nests are made of twigs and cheer,
Chirps and giggles fill the sphere.
A snail races, slow and steady,
In this contest, who's really ready?

Mossy carpets, soft and green,
Hide treasures seldom seen.
A tiny fox plays peek-a-boo,
With a raccoon, it's quite the crew.

Each crevice holds a jest or two,
In this realm where laughter grew.
Secrets dwell in every nook,
In the quiet, life's an open book.

In the Company of Green Guardians

Tall trees stand with knowing grins,
Guardians of the tales that spin.
Their branches dance with playful flair,
As whispers tickle the cool night air.

A raccoon tips its hat with ease,
While owls gossip in the breeze.
Sunlight bursts through leafy gates,
Casting shadows in funny shapes.

Each trunk has a story to share,
Of squirrels, mischief, and silly dare.
Fountains of laughter flow like streams,
In this forest where joy redeems.

With every rustle and soft coo,
The woodland laughs, a joyous crew.
In this haven, humor's the key,
Unlocking nature's sweet decree.

Where the Green Grows Silent

In bushes wide and bold,
Squirrels chitchat loud as gold.
Bees buzz tunes in sunny cheer,
While worms dance without a fear.

A cat prances with a grin,
While leaves whisper tales within.
The breeze carries jokes to share,
Laughter hides just everywhere.

A snail slips by in a race,
Seeking out its special place.
Frogs croak out a funny tune,
As shadows stretch beneath the moon.

In the green, oh what a sight,
Nature plays both day and night.
In this realm of secret glee,
I find joy; it finds me free.

Between the Stems and Silence

In the thicket, secrets tease,
A rabbit sneezes with such ease.
A quail struts in fancy shoes,
While ants parade with no excuse.

The daisies gossip with a wink,
In whispers soft, they share and blink.
The hedgehog rolls in pure delight,
While shadows giggle at the sight.

Beneath a fern, a frog will joke,
A tiny ghost, but made of smoke.
The sunbeams dance with froggy mirth,
Each blade of grass knows its worth.

Giggling leaves sway to and fro,
In the quiet, laughter flows.
Where silliness meets muted grace,
The green grows wild, a happy place.

Ethereal Lines of the Undergrowth

In tangled vines, a jester waits,
To tease the birds through twisted gates.
A hedgehog plays its prickly card,
Yelling jokes that hit quite hard.

Frogs debate the best comic,
While grasshoppers hop with logic.
A snail slides in without a clue,
Saying, "Slimy's in; it's true!"

Butterflies wear silly hats,
Dancing with their amusing spats.
The roots giggle, twisting tight,
As shadows frolic into night.

In the underbrush, we find,
Nature's humor, sweet and blind.
Amidst the green and glee so bold,
A story of laughter unfolds.

Fragments of Quietude

Lost in the green, a joke concealed,
A lizard grins, its fate revealed.
The toad's choir croaks out of tune,
Mocking the stars, a quirky boon.

As daisies chuckle, butterflies sip,
In a floral bar, they share a trip.
Each stem glimmers with giggly charms,
In muddy puddles, the world disarms.

The trees giggle, their bark a grin,
As shadows dance, it's a playful spin.
A squirrel's tail is fluffed with pride,
As woodland critters join the ride.

In quietude, where laughter's crowned,
Hidden happiness all around.
In green realms where hilarity plays,
Nature laughs through all its days.

Lush Borders and Gentle Rhymes

In the garden where gnomes prance,
Laughter hides in each green glance.
A snail slips by with a tiny grin,
Waving hello, let the fun begin.

Cucumbers wearing floppy hats,
Tickling bees, don't forget the chats.
The flowers giggle in vibrant hues,
Dancing with joy in morning dews.

Pansies sing to the fluttering breeze,
While a chubby worm shares jokes with trees.
A daisy winks, oh what a tease!
Spreading humor with utmost ease.

Underneath the sun's warm light,
Every plant joins in delight.
With laughter stitched in nature's seams,
Corn stalks sway to the song of dreams.

The Language of Twisted Roots

Roots that tangle, a comedic sight,
Entwined in punchlines, oh what a fright!
A potato jokes with a witty sprout,
"Why did the carrot explode? No doubt!"

In shadows where thoughts run wild and free,
A radish brags, "I'm the best, you see!"
The turnips exchange their puns with glee,
While beans shoot jokes from their leafy spree.

Underneath the soil, giggles resound,
As worms make puns on what they've found.
In the chaos where all life belongs,
The mud claps hands to nature's songs.

With laughter growing under moon's sight,
The roots intertwine in pure delight.
In this language, both funny and bold,
Every tale of the earth unfolds.

Gossamer Threads of Nature's Pen

Spider spun silk with a twinkling sigh,
Hitching a ride on the breeze passing by.
A ladybug lands with a wink and a cheer,
"Hope you've got snacks, let's party right here!"

Butterflies flutter with glimmers of fun,
Wearing bright jackets under the sun.
They chuckle at ants who march in a line,
"Where's the parade? We've got a good time!"

In the tapestry woven from laughter and light,
Every thread tells a tale, oh what a sight!
The whispers of petals, a soft serenade,
Painting the world in a vibrant charade.

Beneath a wink from the starry night sky,
Nature dances with a merry reply.
In gossamer threads, the world's a sweet jest,
Where critters and blooms laugh and jest.

The Subtle Makeup of Shadows

In the corners where shadows prefer to play,
A sneaky raccoon steals snacks by the bay.
"Who knew the moon would light up my feast?"
He chuckles and munches, a furry little beast!

The sun dips low, painting faces in dark,
As fireflies twinkle and add their spark.
With each little blink, they crack a sly grin,
Dancing in circles, they pull you right in.

There's mischief afoot in the twilight's caress,
As owls tell jokes dressed in their best.
The night hums softly, like tales from afar,
With shadows and giggles beneath every star.

So in the realm where darkness spins round,
All creatures unite in the joy that they've found.
With whispers of laughter, both cheeky and light,
They explore the magic of the soft night.

www.ingramcontent.com/pod-product-compliance
Lightning Source LLC
Chambersburg PA
CBHW052221090526
44585CB00015BA/1353